Published by Tourism East Limited.
PO Box 903. Lilydale VIC 3140, Australia.
www.visityarravalley.com.au
www.visitdandenongranges.com.au
info@yarrarangestourism.com.au

Print Publication ISBN: 978-0-646-71671-8
Digital Publication ISBN: 978-0-646-71672-5

Editor: Gwen Luscombe.
Book design: Christine Better.

The author and publisher have made their best effort ensuring the accuracy of
the information included at the time of publication. They take no responsibility
for change of information, loss, inconvenience or injury incurred by anyone
using this book as a resource, or any business, organisation or individual
featured in this book.

With thanks to Parks Victoria and Visit Victoria for the
additional support and contributions.

Photography courtesy of Parks Victoria, Visit Victoria,
Neisha Breen, Justin Meneguzzi, Yarra Ranges and
Cardinia Council or supplied by subject.

Cover image: Chelsea Australian Garden at Olinda.

CONTENTS:

ACKNOWLEDGEMENT OF COUNTRY:

The gardens included are all part of the Indigenous cultural landscape of the Wurundjeri, Taungurung & Bunurong People of the Kulin Nation on the lands of the world's oldest living culture. Tourism East Limited respects the deep and continuing connection that these Traditional Owners have to these gardens and recognise their role in caring for Country.

This book is a celebration of their ancestral knowledge, expertise and ongoing care they've given to the land, waterways and wildlife. The tourism industry of the Yarra Valley and Dandenong Ranges pay our deepest respects to their Elders, past, present and emerging.

REGION MAP:

CURATED TO ASSIST AND INFORM VISITORS WHILE INSPIRING
VISITATION TO SOME OF OUR KEY GARDENS AND SURROUNDS.

MELBOURNE
AIRPORT

MELBOURNE

YARRA VALLEY

ST ANDREWS
STEELS CREEK
HURSTBRIDGE
DIXONS CREEK
HEALESVILLE
YARRA GLEN
YERING
COLDSTREAM
BROADMEADOWS
KANGAROO
GROUND
GREENSBOROUGH
ELTHAM
LILYDALE
SEVILLE
WOORI
YALLOCK
WARRANDYTE
SOUTH
WANDIN
MOUNT
DANDENONG
RINGWOOD
SASSAFRAS
OLINDA
FERNTREE
GULLY

DANDENONG
RANGES

EMERALD
BELGRAVE
COCKATOO
GEMBROOK

Hume Fwy
Melba Hwy
Eltham Yarra Glen Rd
M80
C726
Metropolitan Ring Rd
Tullamarine Fwy
Ring Rd
Citylink
Maroondah Hwy
Eastern Fwy
East Link
Monash Ferntree Gully Rd
Burwood Hwy
Nepean Hwy
Springvale Rd
East Link
Princess Hwy
Healesville Koo Wee Rup Rd
Monbulk Seville Rd
Pakenham Rd
B380
B3
C411
C424
M1

08
02
17
06
15
11 10
16 13 14
01 07 04
05 09
12

Map Labels

EILDON

Goulburn Valley Hwy

Taggerty-Thornton Rd

Maroondah Hwy

MARYSVILLE

Marysville Rd

LAKE MOUNTAIN

ARBETHONG

WARBURTON

03 18 JUNCTION

GARDENS:

ICONS

Dogs on lead	
Lookout	
Parking	
Waterfall	
Wildlife	
Picnic Spot	
Accommodation	
BBQs	
Cafe	
Changing Places	
Toilets	
Walking	
Retail	
Disability Access	

BILLABONG FALLS, OLINDA

HISTORICAL SIGNIFICANCE:

THE YARRA VALLEY AND DANDENONG RANGES ARE NOT ONLY CELEBRATED FOR THEIR NATURAL BEAUTY BUT ALSO FOR THEIR CULTURAL AND HISTORICAL CONNECTION TO GARDENING, WHICH HAS SHAPED THEIR IDENTITY OVER CENTURIES.

INDIGENOUS ROOTS

The horticultural history of the Yarra Valley and Dandenong Ranges begins with the Wurundjeri, Taungurung and Bunurong people of the Kulin Nation, the traditional custodians of the land. For thousands of years, they've practised sustainable land management and cultivated native plants for food, medicine, and tools. Their intimate knowledge of the local flora and practices contribute to a thriving ecosystem that continues to inspire modern sustainable gardening.

EUROPEAN INFLUENCE AND EARLY SETTLEMENTS

European settlement in the mid-19th century brought significant changes to the landscape. The volcanic fertile soils and temperate climate of the Yarra Valley and Dandenong Ranges made them ideal for agriculture, viticulture, and ornamental horticulture. Settlers introduced exotic plant species and established sprawling gardens that reflected European traditions, blending them with the Australian environment.

This era also saw the establishment of public gardens and arboretums, which became focal points for community gatherings, hospitality and tourism.

THE RISE OF ICONIC GARDENS

By the late 19th and early 20th centuries, the Dandenong Ranges had become synonymous with ornamental gardens. Wealthy landowners and horticultural enthusiasts created grand estates with elaborate gardens that showcased diverse plant collections. Notable examples include the Alfred Nicholas Memorial Gardens and Cloudehill Garden, which exemplify formal garden design while celebrating the natural beauty of the Australian bush.

These gardens were designed not only for aesthetic appeal but also for educational and cultural enrichment. They provided spaces for recreation and inspiration, attracting visitors from Melbourne and beyond. The popularity of these gardens helped establish the Dandenong Ranges as a premier destination for cool climate garden tourism.

THE WINE AND GARDEN CONNECTION

The Yarra Valley, renowned for its wine industry, also boasts a strong connection to horticulture. Vineyards and gardens coexist, with many wineries incorporating beautifully landscaped grounds to enhance the visitor experience. The synergy between viticulture and horticulture highlights the region's dedication to preserving its natural heritage while embracing tourism.

MODERN SIGNIFICANCE

Today, the Yarra Valley and Dandenong Ranges continue to celebrate their horticultural legacy through festivals, garden tours, and conservation efforts. Events such as Tesselaar KaBloom Festival of Flowers and open garden days attract enthusiasts eager to explore the area's botanical wonders. Conservation projects focus on preserving native flora and ensuring that the region's rich horticultural history endures for future generations.

SACRED CONNECTION TO COUNTRY:

THESE LUSH REGIONS ARE HOME TO THE WURUNDJERI, TAUNGURUNG AND BUNURONG PEOPLE, PART OF THE KULIN NATION. THE INDIGENOUS HERITAGE EMBEDDED WITHIN THESE GARDENS REFLECTS A PROFOUND CONNECTION TO THE LAND, UNDERPINNED BY TRADITIONS, KNOWLEDGE SYSTEMS, AND SUSTAINABLE PRACTICES.

The gardens, waterways and forests of the Yarra Valley and Dandenong Ranges are more than scenic retreats – they are sacred Country imbued with spiritual, cultural, and ecological meaning. These lands are considered living entities. The waterways, plants, and animals form an interconnected system providing sustenance and spiritual guidance.

Many of the plants found in these areas were integral to the Wurundjeri way of life, used for food, medicine, tools, and ceremonial purposes. Native species such as the Murnong (yam daisy) were cultivated as a food source, while eucalyptus and tea trees had medicinal uses. Native plants such as wattle, cherry ballart and manna gum utilised for smoking ceremonies.

The gardens also provided habitats for animals like kangaroos and possums, which were hunted for food and materials in a manner that maintained ecological balance.

Some historic gardens in the region contain sites where important ceremonies, gatherings, and storytelling took place. These locations remain vital to the cultural identity of the Wurundjeri people.

The arrival of European settlers in the 19th century brought significant disruption to Indigenous stewardship of the Yarra Valley and Dandenong Ranges. Land clearing for agriculture and development, coupled with the introduction of non-native plants, transformed the landscape. Many sacred sites were altered or lost, and traditional knowledge systems were marginalised. However, remnants of Indigenous practices and knowledge persist, often interwoven with the introduced elements of historic gardens.

In recent years, there has been a growing recognition of the Indigenous significance of the historic gardens in the Yarra Valley and Dandenong Ranges. Collaborative efforts between local Wurundjeri communities and conservation groups aim to restore traditional knowledge and practices to these landscapes. Projects that incorporate Indigenous land management techniques, cultural interpretation, and educational initiatives are fostering a deeper appreciation of the region's heritage.

17: WURUNDJERI WALK, HEALESVILLE SANCTUARY

OUR COOL CLIMATE GARDENS:

GARDENS IN THE YARRA VALLEY & DANDENONG RANGES ARE RENOWNED FOR THEIR UNIQUE BEAUTY, LUSH DIVERSITY, AND THE SEASONAL SPECTACLE THEY OFFER. THE COOLER TEMPERATURES, HIGHER ALTITUDES, AND AMPLE RAINFALL OF THE REGION CREATE IDEAL CONDITIONS FOR A VARIETY OF PLANT SPECIES AND FOSTER A THRIVING ECOSYSTEM FOR BOTH NATIVE AUSTRALIAN PLANTS AND EXOTIC SPECIES.

One defining feature of these gardens is the way they change with the seasons. In spring, the gardens burst into life, showcasing vibrant blossoms and the fresh green of new growth. Rhododendrons, azaleas, and magnolias are common highlights, with their brilliant colours attracting both visitors and local wildlife. Summer brings dense foliage and a lush, verdant canopy, providing cool, shaded spaces that are particularly inviting. Autumn is one of the most spectacular times to visit when the maple, elm and oak leaves transform into warm hues of red, orange, and yellow, creating a breathtaking display of colour. Finally, winter showcases the intricate textures and forms of bare branches, mosses, and hardy evergreens, often dusted with frost in the early morning hours.

The cool climate of the Yarra Valley and Dandenong Ranges also supports rare and unusual plants, from giant tree ferns to delicate hellebores and graceful Japanese maples. This diversity attracts garden enthusiasts, botanists, and casual visitors alike, as they can experience plant varieties and species not commonly seen elsewhere in Australia.

Beyond botanical appeal, these gardens offer a serene escape into nature, ideal for reflection and relaxation. Visitors can wander through landscaped paths, enjoy the views, and immerse themselves in the sounds and scents of nature. Our beautiful and biodiverse gardens also play a role in conservation and environmental education, as many gardens in the area are committed to preserving native plants and showcasing sustainable gardening practices.

We invite you to explore our region in all seasons and discover why it's so special.

YARRA VALLEY, VICTORIA

PHOTOGRAPHING OUR GARDENS:

VISITING OUR STUNNING FLORAL GARDENS IS A VISUAL TREAT FOR NATURE LOVERS AND PHOTOGRAPHERS ALIKE AND ARE HOME TO SOME OF VICTORIA'S MOST BREATHTAKING DISPLAYS OF SEASONAL BLOOMS, FROM VIBRANT RHODODENDRONS TO DELICATE CHERRY BLOSSOMS.

Whether you're wandering through the manicured landscapes of the Dandenong Ranges Botanic Garden or capturing wildflowers in a hidden valley, the opportunity to photograph nature at its most colorful and serene is one not to miss. To help you make the most of your garden photography experience, here are five essential tips:

SHOOT DURING GOLDEN HOURS

Capture photos early in the morning or late in the afternoon when the sunlight is soft and warm. This avoids harsh shadows and helps colours pop.

USE A SHALLOW DEPTH OF FIELD

Use a wide aperture (like f/2.8 to f/5.6) to blur the background and make the flowers stand out sharply against a soft, dreamy backdrop.

MIND THE COMPOSITION

Apply the rule of thirds, look for leading lines like garden paths, and avoid cluttered backgrounds. Get low or try unique angles to create more dynamic shots.

FOCUS ON DETAILS

Zoom in on interesting textures, patterns, or individual blooms. Water droplets, bees, or petals in sunlight can add drama and interest.

WATCH THE WIND

Even a slight breeze can blur flowers. Use faster shutter speeds or wait for still moments. Alternatively, bring a wind block or shoot on calm days.

PIRIANDA GARDENS, OLINDA

07: DANDENONG RANGES BOTANIC GARDEN

07: DANDENONG RANGES BOTANIC GARDEN

NOTABLE PEOPLE:

OUR REGION'S VIBRANT HORTICULTURAL LANDSCAPES ARE SHAPED NOT ONLY BY NATURE BUT THE VISION AND DEDICATION OF REMARKABLE INDIVIDUALS.

This section highlights some of the most notable people whose passion, innovation, and hard work have enriched the region's gardens, parks, and plant life. Their lasting contributions continue to inspire and cultivate a deeper appreciation for the natural beauty of this unique part of Victoria.

EDNA WALLING:

A pioneer of Australian Landscape Design, Edna Walling (1895–1973) was one of Australia's most celebrated landscape designers, whose work significantly influenced the development of horticulture and garden design in Australia. Her contributions, particularly to the Yarra Valley & Dandenong Ranges have remained an enduring legacy.

Immigrating to Australia from England with her family as a teenager in 1914, Walling studied horticulture at Burnley Horticultural College in Melbourne, graduating in 1917. This education laid the foundation for her innovative approach to landscape design, where she sought to harmonise human-made structures with the natural environment.

Walling's career blossomed in the 1920s and 1930s as she began creating gardens in Melbourne and regional Victoria for prominent homes including for Elisabeth Murdoch, Sir Frank Packer and Dame Nellie Melba's Yarra Valley home at Coombe.

Her designs were heavily influenced by the English Arts and Crafts movement, which emphasised the integration of architecture and garden spaces. However, Walling adapted this ethos to suit the Australian climate, promoting the use of native plants and water-wise gardening techniques long before sustainability became a global concern.

The Yarra Valley & Dandeong Ranges became a key site of Walling's work and inspiration. She created numerous gardens in the area, blending its natural beauty with her signature style. Her projects often included stonework pathways, low stone walls, and informal garden layouts that mimicked the natural bushland. Walling believed in preserving the native flora and used local plants such as wattles, eucalypts, and grevilleas to maintain a sense of place.

Walling's contributions extended beyond individual gardens. In the 1920s, she purchased land in Mooroolbark, where she established a unique residential village called Bickleigh Vale. The development, named after a village in Devon, England, showcased her vision of harmonious living. Each cottage was surrounded by a thoughtfully designed garden, creating a cohesive and picturesque community that exists to this day and is recognised by The National Trust and declared an area of special significance by the Yarra Ranges Shire Council.

Walling left Bickleigh Vale for Queensland in 1967. Property owners – now 'Friends of Edna Walling' – became caretakers of the village, and today it's a thriving community.

Walling's influence wasn't limited to her designs; Walling was also a prolific writer and photographer. She contributed articles to magazines such as Australian Home Beautiful, inspiring a generation of gardeners and designers. Her books, including Gardens in Australia (1943) and A Gardener's Log (1948), are still referenced for their wisdom and philosophy.

Edna Walling's work not only enhanced the region's aesthetic but also underscored the importance of preserving the natural landscape. Her pioneering use of native plants set the stage for contemporary Australian garden design, which continues to celebrate biodiversity and sustainability.

Today, her legacy is celebrated through preserved gardens and historical sites. Her philosophy of working with nature rather than against it remains relevant in the face of modern environmental challenges. Edna Walling's vision transformed Australian horticulture, leaving a timeless imprint on the Yarra Ranges and beyond.

While there is no public access to the gardens at Bickleigh Vale, Open Gardens Victoria regularly hosts events opening private gardens to the public. Bickleigh Vale is regularly featured as part of the Open Gardens program in October.

Visitors can park on Pembroke Road and respectfully stroll the lanes, but are kindly asked to respect the privacy of residents and not attempt to access the gardens outside of Open Garden days.

TESSELAAR FAMILY:

In June 1939 – weeks before the outbreak of World War 2 in Europe – Cees and Johanna Tesselaar left Holland for Australia aboard the Strathallan on their wedding day.

They first settled in Ferntree Gully, before moving to Silvan in 1945. They purchased a six-hectare farm and planted their first crop of tulips and gladioli. Over the following decades, the company, Padua Bulb Nurseries, became Australia's largest family-owned floricultural operation.

The company's industry leadership is enhanced through a long-standing commitment to developing the industry as a whole. This tradition began in the 1940s and '50s with Cees Tesselaar helping other Dutch immigrants establish their own nursery businesses. Now headed by the 'larger Tesselaar family' – its employees, Tesselaar is a unique blend of the growing and marketing of cut flowers, bulbs, plants and perennials. The major thrust of the business is the distribution of flowers grown on the Tesselaar farms situated around the country. Through a specialist network of subsidiaries and associate companies around Australia, locally grown flowers are air freighted and delivered directly to florists around the country.

As most cut flowers are grown under cover, Tesselaar's pioneered the use of plastic houses in Australia back in the 1960s. Now with six hectares under cover, including the latest automatic elevated houses, the world's most fuel-efficient computerised glasshouse system, Tesselaar's can consistently grow year-round.

Amongst the first to see the potential of mail ordering as a powerful distribution method, Tesselaar is now the largest bulb and perennial mail order company in Australia with a large and loyal customer base. Tesselaar family members have also participated in tourism, training, floricultural and horticultural organisations, including serving as president of both the Nursery Industry Association of Victoria and Flower Growers Association of Victoria. They've been on the boards of the Nursery Industry Association of Australia, the Horticultural Research and Development Council, the Australian Flower Export Council, the Australian Flower Growers Council, the local tourism authority and they participate in the Industry Training Council Board of Victoria.

As passersby regularly stopped for roadside photographs of the blooming fields each spring and autumn, the family opened their farm to the public for two special events. The annual Tesselaar Tulip Festival and KaBloom Festival of Flowers, both held at the Silvan farm in September/October and late March/April, respectively, celebrate the family heritage with fields packed with more than three million blooms, including 10,000 sqm of wildflowers for KaBloom. The award-winning festivals draw in visitors by the thousands to enjoy the explosions of colour, circus performances, food, activities and more.

JEREMY FRANCIS:

Local master gardener, Jeremy Francis has profoundly influenced horticulture in the Yarra Valley and Dandenong Ranges through his creation and stewardship of Cloudehill Gardens. Jeremy's passion for gardening was ignited after a chance meeting with British gardener Christopher Lloyd. This encounter led him to the Dandenong Ranges in the early 1990s, where he sought land to cultivate a garden. In 1992, he acquired a historic two-hectare property in Olinda, previously a flower farm and nursery established by the Woolrich family in the 1920s.

Recognising the site's potential, he embarked on an ambitious journey to transform the overgrown landscape into a masterpiece of cool-climate gardening. He meticulously designed the garden's structure, incorporating a central axis flanked by formal clipped hedges, topiaries, and relaxed bulb meadows. His approach combined careful planning with spontaneous creativity to sculpt the land in alignment with his vision.

Under Jeremy's guidance, Cloudehill Gardens flourished into a horticultural haven, showcasing a diverse array of rare plants, including venerable beech trees, weeping Japanese maples, and Himalayan tree rhododendrons. The garden's design pays homage to classic European styles, featuring elements such as a green circular 'theatre' space reminiscent of Roman and Greek gardens.

In 2013, Jeremy collaborated with The Diggers Club, a renowned gardening organisation, to enhance Cloudehill's offerings. While retaining ownership and control of the garden, he entrusted the nursery operations to Diggers, aligning with their shared dedication to "garden worthiness" and sustainable practices.

Beyond his work in the garden, Jeremy authored "Cloudehill: A Year in the Garden," a comprehensive book detailing the garden's evolution, enriched with photographs by Claire Takacs.

Jeremy's unwavering dedication and innovative approach have cemented Cloudehill Gardens as a cornerstone of horticultural excellence in the Yarra Valley and Dandenong Ranges, inspiring gardeners and nature enthusiasts alike.

SUE FORRESTER & BILL MOLYNEUX:

The Burrow at Wombat Bend, a unique nature retreat in Dixon's Creek, has been shaped by the dedication and passion of its owners. Deeply influenced by their lifelong love of Australian flora and the environment, they have created a thriving wildlife habitat that seamlessly integrates nature and hospitality.

Sue's connection to landscape design began in childhood at Bickleigh Vale, a heritage-listed village in Mooroolbark, Victoria, created by renowned garden designer Edna Walling. Her mother, Gwynnyth Crouch, worked closely with Walling for a decade before building the family cottage, Wimborne. This early exposure to natural beauty fostered Sue's deep appreciation for plants. Bill's formative years exploring Melbourne's western plains and working as a jackaroo in the Riverina region of New South Wales strengthened his passion for Australian flora and conservation. Together, Sue and Bill established Austraflora Nursery in Montrose, Victoria, in the early 1970s, promoting Australian native plants in garden design. They travelled extensively across Australia – from Tasmania to the Kimberley and Victoria's High Country – seeking new plants suited to horticulture and landscape design. These wide-ranging expeditions inspired their work in horticulture, and they have co-authored over 25 scientific papers on new plant species, published in Muelleria, the journal of the Royal Botanic Gardens, Victoria.

At Wombat Bend, they continue to develop drought-resistant and heat-tolerant native plant varieties suited to contemporary landscaping needs. Their commitment extends beyond their own property, as they also design sustainable landscapes, featuring exclusively Australian flora. The heart of Wombat Bend is its billabong, a thriving ecosystem supporting diverse birdlife and wildlife. Wombat Bend is a Land for Wildlife sanctuary and Sue and Bill's deep love for animals is reflected in their tireless work with Airedale Terrier Rescue & Adoption and wildlife rescue, particularly wombats. Sharing the beauty of Wombat Bend is integral to their vision. Their self-contained bed and breakfast, The Burrow, offers guests a tranquil retreat and a chance to reconnect with nature. Many visitors return regularly, drawn to the serenity and immersive experience of the natural surroundings. Wombat Bend is more than a home; it is a sustainable living landscape, a sanctuary of native flora and fauna, and a testament to the enduring commitment of its creators. Their passion remains undiminished, with each day offering new opportunities to cultivate and share their love of the Australian environment.

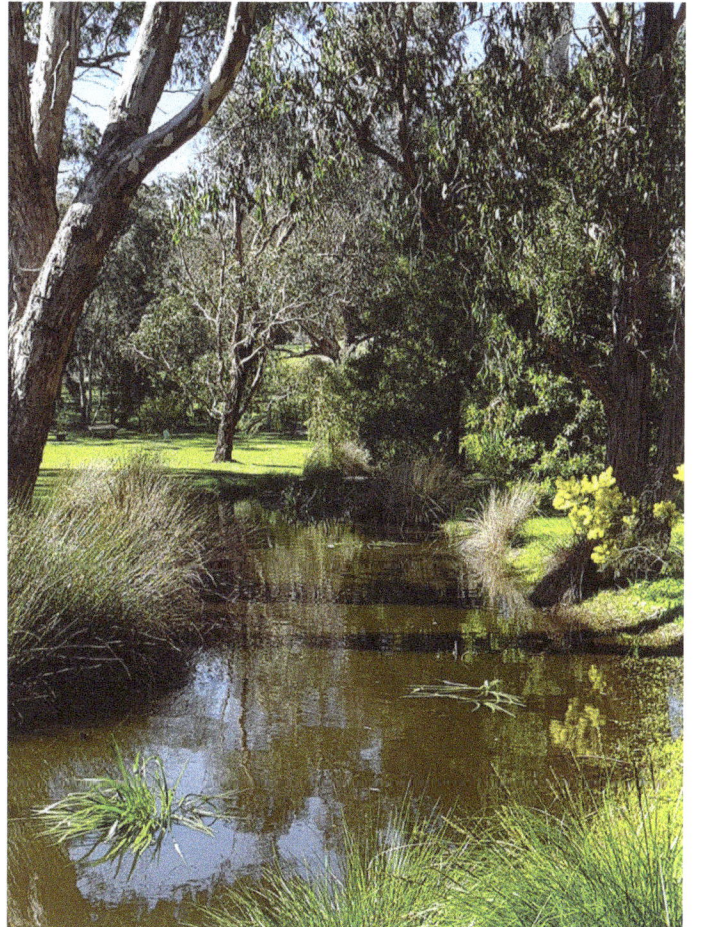

PHILLIP JOHNSON:

Through his innovative and sustainable designs, distinguished Australian landscape designer Phillip Johnson, has profoundly influenced garden tourism and landscape design in the Yarra Valley and Dandenong Ranges. His work emphasises the integration of natural elements, creating harmonious environments that foster a deep connection between people and nature.

In 2013, Johnson achieved international acclaim when his 'Trailfinders Australian Garden' won the prestigious Best in Show award at the Chelsea Flower Show. This groundbreaking design highlighted the beauty and resilience of Australian native plants, capturing the attention of a global audience. The garden's success underscored the potential for sustainable, native-focused landscaping to resonate on an international stage.

Building upon this success, Johnson embarked on an ambitious project to recreate the award-winning Chelsea garden within the Dandenong Ranges Botanic Garden in Olinda. This endeavor, known as the Chelsea Australian Garden at Olinda, spans over 7,000 square meters — making it twenty eight times larger than the original exhibit. The garden features more than 15,000 plants representing over 400 Australian species, including rare and endangered varieties. Designed with sustainability at its core, the garden incorporates solar power and water-wise principles, serving as a living testament to his commitment to ecological harmony.

Johnson's influence extends beyond public spaces to private residences as well. His former home, Billabong Falls, located in the heart of the Dandenong Ranges, has been transformed into a luxurious bed and breakfast. Guests can immerse themselves in the serene landscape, surrounded by natural bushland and the soothing sounds of cascading water. This retreat exemplifies Johnson's ability to create spaces that offer both aesthetic beauty and a restorative connection to nature. The property features a natural swimming pool, lush native gardens, and is enveloped by towering Mountain Ash trees, offering filtered views of the Yarra Valley. This space not only reflects his design philosophy but also provides an immersive experience for guests, showcasing the potential of sustainable landscaping.

Through his visionary designs and unwavering dedication to sustainability, Phillip Johnson has left an indelible mark on the region by not only enhancing the region's natural beauty but also inspiring a broader appreciation for environmentally conscious landscape design.

Images by: Phillip Johnson and Claire Takacsto.

KABLOOM FESTIVAL OF FLOWERS

Gardens of the Yarra Valley & Dandenong Ranges

EVENTS, FESTIVALS AND SEASONAL ACTIVITIES:

VISITING THE REGION IN ANY SEASON IS ALWAYS SPECTACULAR, ESPECIALLY DURING VIBRANT HORTICULTURAL EVENTS. AMONG THESE, THE TESSELAAR KABLOOM FESTIVAL, TESSELAAR TULIP FESTIVAL, AND OPEN GARDENS VICTORIA STAND OUT, OFFERING VISITORS IMMERSIVE EXPERIENCES AMIDST BREATHTAKING FLORAL DISPLAYS.

TESSELAAR KABLOOM FESTIVAL OF FLOWERS

Held annually at the Tesselaar Flower Farm in Silvan, the KaBloom Festival is a celebration of nature's autumnal beauty. Spanning from late March to late April, this festival transforms a 25-acre working farm into a vibrant tapestry of color, showcasing hundreds of thousands of blooming flowers. Visitors can wander through expansive fields filled with a diverse array of blooms, creating a mesmerising and immersive floral experience. Beyond the visual spectacle, the festival offers live entertainment, ensuring enjoyment for all ages. With delicious food stalls, tractor rides, and various family-friendly activities, the KaBloom Festival provides a delightful day out in the Dandenong Ranges.

TESSELAAR TULIP FESTIVAL

Having started in 1954, each spring, from mid-September to mid-October, the Tesselaar Tulip Festival captivates visitors with over a million blooming tulips. It offers a kaleidoscope of colors and a rich cultural experience.

Themed weekends enhance the festivities, celebrating various cultures and interests including Dutch and Turkish Weekends honoring the tulip's origins in Turkey and reflecting the heritage of the Tesselaar family's Dutch heritage. Themed weekends include traditional music, dance, food and cultural experiences. Additionally, weekends dedicated to food, wine and jazz or Children's Weeks, designed for younger visitors are popular, featuring activities, performances, and opportunities to learn about nature and gardening.

The festival not only offers stunning floral displays but also provides live entertainment, market stalls, and the chance to experience different cultures in a vibrant setting.

Both the Tesselaar KaBloom and Tulip Festival are ticketed events.

OPEN GARDENS VICTORIA

Open Gardens Victoria (OGV) is a not-for-profit organisation dedicated to opening private gardens to the public, fostering a love for gardening and appreciation for green spaces. Throughout the year, OGV curates a program of garden openings across Victoria, including the Yarra Valley and Dandenong Ranges. These events offer visitors a unique opportunity to explore diverse garden designs, gain inspiration, and engage with passionate gardeners. Proceeds from these openings often support charitable causes, horticultural projects, and community initiatives, making each visit both enjoyable and impactful.

One notable event is the opening of the Bickleigh Vale Village, a storybook village established by renowned architect Edna Walling. Visitors can stroll through enchanting gardens, each reflecting Walling's design principles, and experience the harmony between architecture and landscape. The OGV website regularly lists upcoming events and ticketing information.

Collectively, these festivals and open gardens highlight the region's rich horticultural heritage and provide visitors with immersive experiences that celebrate the beauty and diversity of plant life.

DANDENONG RANGES BOTANIC GARDEN, OLINDA

Gardens of the Yarra Valley & Dandenong Ranges

SEASONAL HIGHLIGHTS:

THE YARRA VALLEY AND DANDENONG RANGES ARE HOME TO SOME OF VICTORIA'S MOST CAPTIVATING COOL-CLIMATE GARDENS, OFFERING UNIQUE SEASONAL HIGHLIGHTS THROUGHOUT THE YEAR.

Here's a guide to what you can expect in each season:

SPRING (SEPTEMBER – NOVEMBER)

A vibrant time to visit, our gardens are bursting into bloom over the spring:

- **Dandenong Ranges Botanic Garden (Olinda):** This garden showcases over 15,000 rhododendrons, 12,000 azaleas, 3,000 camellias, and 250,000 daffodils, creating a spectacular floral display. Cherry blossoms also add to the springtime charm.
- **R.J. Hamer Arboretum:** Early flowering species line the walking tracks, offering spectacular views across the Yarra Valley and Warburton Ranges.
- **Chelsea Australian Garden at Olinda:** Located within the Dandenong Ranges Botanic Garden, this garden features over 15,000 plants, including 400 different Australian species, and is particularly vibrant in spring.

AUTUMN (MARCH – MAY)

Autumn brings a rich tapestry of colours as foliage turns:

- **Dandenong Ranges Botanic Garden:** The garden's deciduous trees display brilliant autumn hues, making it a favourite spot for photography and leisurely walks.
- **Alfred Nicholas Memorial Garden:** Famous for its ornamental lake and iconic boathouse, this garden offers beautiful autumn foliage amidst its historic landscape.
- **Pirianda Garden:** Featuring a variety of deciduous trees that provide a spectacular autumn display, complemented by its serene setting, this garden is particularly special in autumn.

WINTER (JUNE – AUGUST)

Winter offers a serene beauty, with some gardens showcasing unique features:

- **Dandenong Ranges Botanic Garden:** Even in winter, the garden's structure and design provide a tranquil experience, with the possibility of witnessing snow-dusted landscapes.
- **R.J. Hamer Arboretum:** The arboretum's collection of conifers and deciduous trees offers a peaceful winter landscape, ideal for quiet walks.

SUMMER (DECEMBER – FEBRUARY)

Summer is perfect for exploring shaded areas and enjoying the lush greenery:

- **Cloudehill Gardens:** This garden boasts a series of garden rooms with a variety of plants that thrive in summer, providing a cool retreat.
- **Mount Dandenong Arboretum:** Featuring a collection of maturing deciduous trees and conifers, the arboretum offers shaded paths and a diverse range of tree species.

Each season in the Yarra Valley and Dandenong Ranges offers a unique and beautiful garden experience. Whether you're seeking vibrant blooms, autumnal colours, serene winter landscapes, or lush summer greenery, there's always something to enjoy.

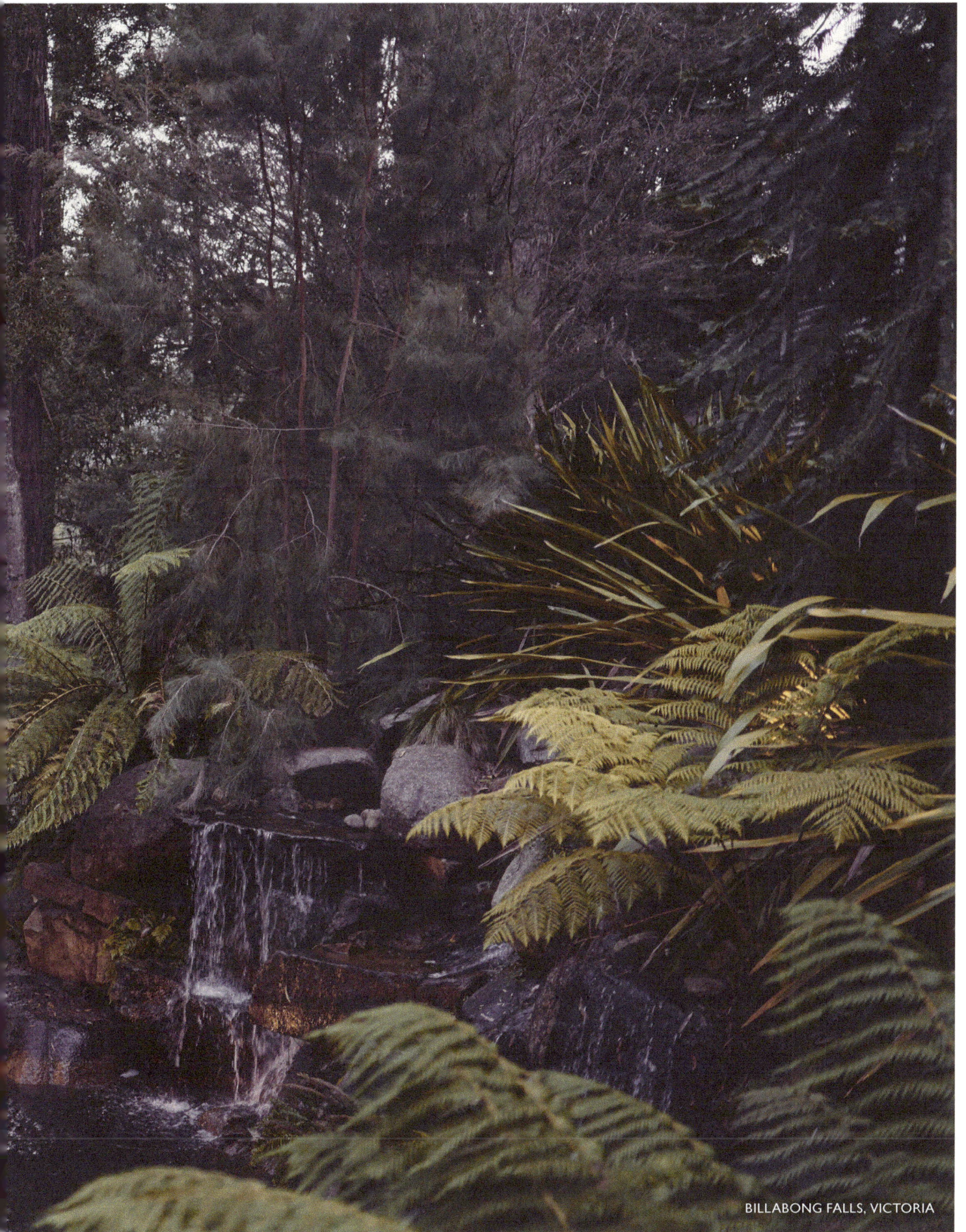

BILLABONG FALLS, VICTORIA

GARDENS:

BEFORE YOU VISIT: YOUR SAFETY IS PARAMOUNT.

OUR PARKS AND GARDENS ARE BEAUTIFUL PLACES TO VISIT THROUGHOUT THE YEAR, BUT IT'S ESSENTIAL TO BE MINDFUL OF THE FIRE DANGER RATINGS OR SEVERE WEATHER EVENTS BEFORE YOU ARRIVE.

These ratings will affect accessibility into the parks and gardens. In some cases of fire risk or severe weather, gardens may be closed for safety.

Newer gardens, such as the Chelsea Australia Native Garden at Olinda, include an integrated bushfire protection system, but for visitor safety, will still close on days of Extreme Fire Danger Rating or severe weather events.

Plants and flowers within the gardens are protected. Keep our gardens beautiful by leaving them for others to enjoy and always take your rubbish with you (if bins are not available).

Not all gardens are pet-suitable, some will allow for dogs on lead only. Assistance dogs are allowed and for gardens within national parks, permits may be required for assistance dogs.

01:

ALFRED NICHOLAS MEMORIAL GARDEN

1A SHERBROOKE ROAD, SHERBROOKE

The original garden of the historic Burnham Beeches Estate, Alfred Nicholas Memorial Garden is incredibly picturesque. Named in honour of pharmaceutical businessman and philanthropist, Alfred Nicholas, an avid horticulturalist who established several gardens including Burnham Beeches in 1929. Meticulously designed by Cornish landscaper Percival Trevaskis, it was filled with a wide range of plants, including some purchased by Nicholas at Chelsea Flower Show that same year. Well-photographed and much admired for its ornamental lake and footbridges, an iconic boatshed, multiple water features, garden sculpture and pathways that weave under a towering canopy of Mountain Ash trees, this garden offers something to enjoy in every season. Spring brings flower cherries, rhododendrons, camellias and azaleas while Autumn sees a beautiful spectrum of colourful foliage and the famous golden ginkgos along the lake. The summer months see the native ferns, fuchsia, hydrangeas and orchids fill the garden with colour and even winter visitors will enjoy camellias.

As a family-favourite, bring a picnic, take a scenic stroll down the sloped pathway to the lake where the iconic boathouse sits just waiting to be photographed. Enjoy the surrounding birdsong; here you'll find king parrots, rosellas, kookaburras and of course, ducks on the lake. Alfred Nicholas Memorial Garden is managed and maintained by Parks Victoria.

WHEN: Daily from 10am to 5pm, closed Christmas Day.
COST: Free.

01: ALFRED NICHOLAS MEMORIAL GARDEN

02:

ALOWYN GARDENS AND NURSERY

1230 MELBA HIGHWAY, YARRA GLEN

The award-winning Alowyn Gardens and Nursery offers nine distinctly different and beautifully landscaped gardens set over seven acres. Following its transformation from a trotting farm, into an award-winning display garden, the owners were named by the ABC's Gardening Australia as Gardeners of the Year in 2008. The transformation to nationally recognised garden showcases the dedication and vision of the garden's creators over a relatively short timeframe, truly a true labour of love for its owners, landscaper John and horticulturalist Prue since 1997.

In particular, their Birch Forest features 400 closely-planted birch trees, an unusual and distinctive landscape feature that's quite remarkable - and creates a unique microenvironment, bird habitat and visual experience that's atypical of Australian garden settings.

Popular with garden enthusiasts, photographers and families alike, the kid-friendly labyrinth maze is a hit with kids. Picnics are allowed in the gardens and a kiosk cafe are particularly popular when the Wisteria is in bloom for roughly four weeks in mid-October.

The onsite nursery and greenhouse is fully stocked with a wide variety of indoor and outdoor plants and garden supplies. Alowyn Gardens is privately-owned and maintained.

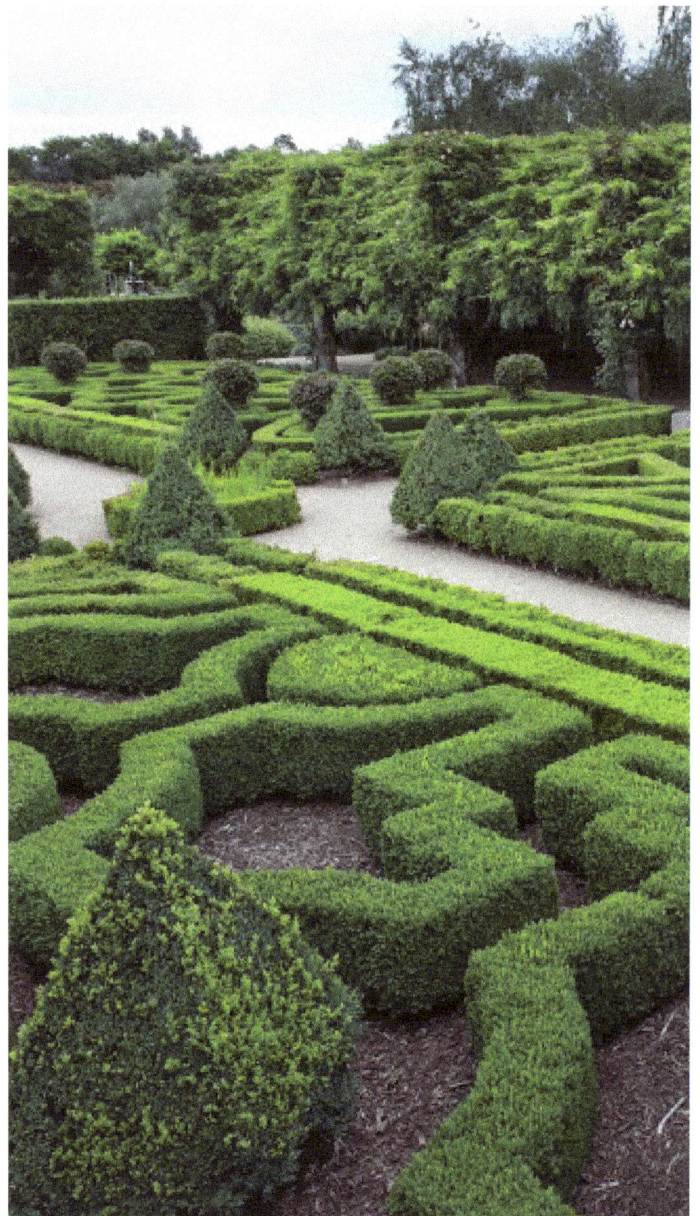

WHEN: Daily from 10am to 5pm excluding Christmas Day and Boxing Day. Onsite weddings may require a 4pm closure.

COST: Cafe and nursery access is free. Gardens are ticketed. Children under 12 are free.

03:

BLUE LOTUS WATER GARDEN

2628 WARBURTON HIGHWAY, YARRA JUNCTION

Open from Boxing Day until mid-April each year, the tropically-themed Blue Lotus Water Garden is a spectacular seasonal garden open to the public. The opening season makes it quite unique as it's specifically designed around the flowering seasons of its exotic plants, rather than being a year-round attraction like most botanical gardens. The 14-acre water garden features millions of beautiful lotus, waterlily and other flowers, as well as attractions such as giant Amazon waterlilies, Lotus Lake, flower fairy gardens, Cochrane's Lake Bridge walk, a Claude Monet waterlily display and much more.

Visitors particularly enjoy their Giant Amazon Waterlilies which produce huge white flowers over 30cm in size before gradually turning pink and withering within 48 hours. This color transformation and short flowering cycle makes timing a visit quite special as visitors might witness completely different colored blooms depending on when they arrive.

Each year the garden holds two must-see floral events, starting with the famous Lotus Flower Season (26th Dec – 20th March) followed by their Autumn Flower Season (21st March – mid April). Inside the garden you will find a host of fantastic facilities including picnic areas, play grounds and a lovely cafe. It's visually stunning and memorable day out. The Blue Lotus Water Garden is privately owned and maintained.

WHEN: 26th December to mid-April.

COST: Garden and facilities access is ticketed, children admitted free (conditions apply).

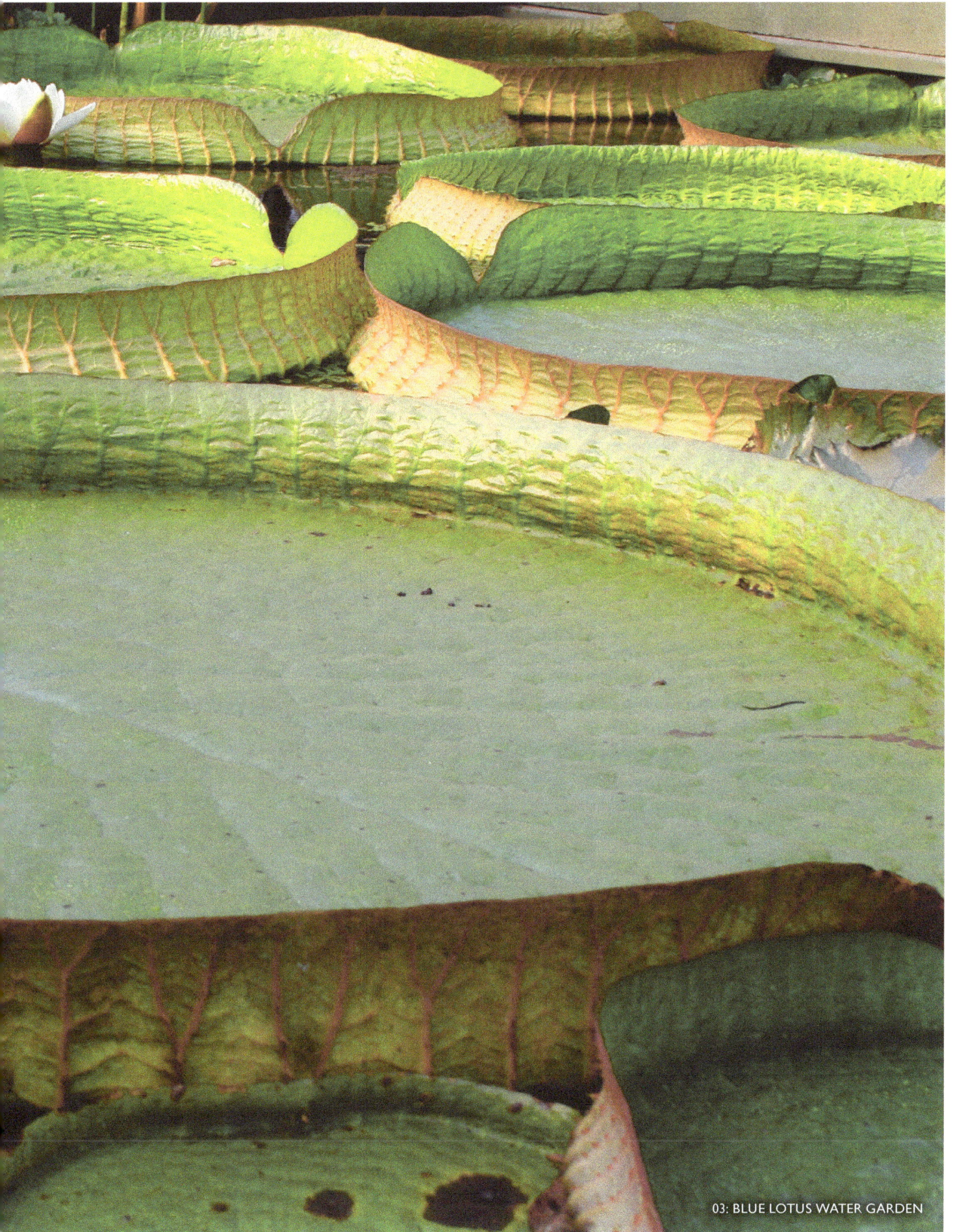

03: BLUE LOTUS WATER GARDEN

04:

CHELSEA AUSTRALIAN GARDEN

24 THE GEORGIAN ROAD, DANDENONG RANGES BOTANIC GARDEN, OLINDA

The 'Australian Garden' display by Phillip Johnson, Wes Fleming and the Trailfinders team became the first ever Australian entry to win at the 2013 Royal Horticultural Society's Chelsea Flower Show. Unanimously voted 'Best in Show' and toured by the late Queen and Prince Harry, the display has since been permanently re-created at 20 times the size within the Dandenong Ranges Botanic Garden. More than 150,000 plants have been used, including 400+ Australian species. Transforming what was once a golf course, into a glorious garden with several rare and endangered plants, an enormous 9 metre Waratah sculpture, waterfall and billabong, both providing a native habitat for native animals.

The Chelsea Australian Garden at Olinda also features 22 incredibly ancient Wollemi Pines, some close to 3 metres in height, from the Royal Botanic Gardens in NSW. Once thought to be extinct and then rediscovered in the NSW Blue Mountains in 1994. Often called 'living fossils', this garden is home to one of the most significant collections of the prehistoric species. Paths throughout this spectacular garden are sealed and offer the perfect opportunity to enjoy the birdsong or enjoy a picnic on the lawn under a Boab tree. The Chelsea Australian Garden at Olinda is maintained and managed by Parks Victoria.

Images by: Phil Johnson and Claire Takacsto.

WHEN: Daily from 10am to 5pm, closed Christmas Day.
COST: Free.

05:
CLOUDEHILL GARDENS & NURSERY

89 OLINDA-MONBULK ROAD, OLINDA

Set out over ten acres in Olinda, Cloudhill Gardens & Nursery comprises 25 garden compartments and also a substantial 100 year old woodland great for children to explore. Placed throughout the garden is an incredible collection of artwork, featuring a variety of Australian artists in a variety of mediums.

Popular for weddings year round, each season brings something new to enjoy, but depending on the time of year, expect to discover peony gardens, a spring shrub walk, bluebell woodlands, extensive bulb and weeping Japanese maples at the heart of the garden. Imported from Japan's legendary Yokohama Nursery, they have been growing on the property since 1928.

Throughout the year, special events are held within the gardens including theatre performances in the amphitheatre.

The onsite Diggers Club Garden shop offers a wide range of Diggers Club heritage fruit and vegetables, and rare and outstanding herbaceous perennials. Also visit Jeff Barry's 'Chojo Nursery' to see his collection of some of the best bonsais in the world outside Japan.

Cloudehill Gardens & Nursery is privately owned and maintained.

WHEN: Daily from 10am to 5pm.

COST: Garden access is ticketed for adults 16+, children and Diggers Club members are free.

06:

COOMBE YARRA VALLEY

673-675 MAROONDAH HIGHWAY, COLDSTREAM

Established in 1909 as the private home of Australia's beloved opera soprano star, Dame Nellie Melba, Coombe Yarra Valley has taken its name after a house she rented in England while performing at Covent Garden.

Coombe Cottage remains the private residence of Melba's family and was the home of her granddaughter, Pamela Lady Vestey, until her passing in 2011. Visitors can step behind the famous hedges to tour the cottage and seven acres of gardens designed by William Guilfoyle, the renowned architect of Melbourne's Royal Botanic Gardens.

Additionally, the gardens feature one of Victoria's oldest swimming pools, also designed by Guilfoyle, adding another layer of historical importance to the property beyond its famous association with Melba. The tour showcases rare plants, terraced lawns, rose arbour, croquet lawn and more. Tours last about an hour, guiding you through this enchanting setting.

Visit Coombe Cottage, preserved in its original condition, to get a glimpse into Melba's opulent life. While there, indulge in estate-grown wines at the cellar door, or enjoy lunch at the restaurant, serving the iconic Peach Melba dessert, created in Melba's honour. Coombe Yarra Valley is privately owned and maintained.

WHEN: Open Wednesday to Sunday, closed Good Friday and Christmas Day.
COST: Tours are ticketed, bookings required.

07:

DANDENONG RANGES BOTANIC GARDEN

24 THE GEORGIAN ROAD, OLINDA

Featuring an extensive collection of rhododendrons, azaleas, camellias, daffodils and more, the Dandenong Ranges Botanic Garden is a delight to visit in all seasons.

Formerly known as the National Rhododendron Garden, this garden houses Australia's largest collection of Australian and overseas raised hybrids of rhododendrons that cannot be replaced, re-bred or re-imported. Featuring a collection of 15,000 rhododendrons is not just impressive in size, but irreplaceable in terms of botanical heritage as visitors are experiencing unique hybrid varieties that literally cannot be found or recreated anywhere else in the world.

Wander the pathways that highlight the ever-changing landscape, enjoy a leisurely lunch at the onsite cafes or bring a picnic basket to enjoy on one of the lawns. Browse the gift shop, buy a ticket for the Garden Explorer, a people mover providing a 25-minute tour of the garden or make your way to Serenity Point offering stunning views over the Yarra Ranges and beyond.

The Dandenong Ranges Botanic Garden is maintained and managed by Parks Victoria.

WHEN: Daily from 10am to 5pm, closed Christmas Day.
COST: Free.

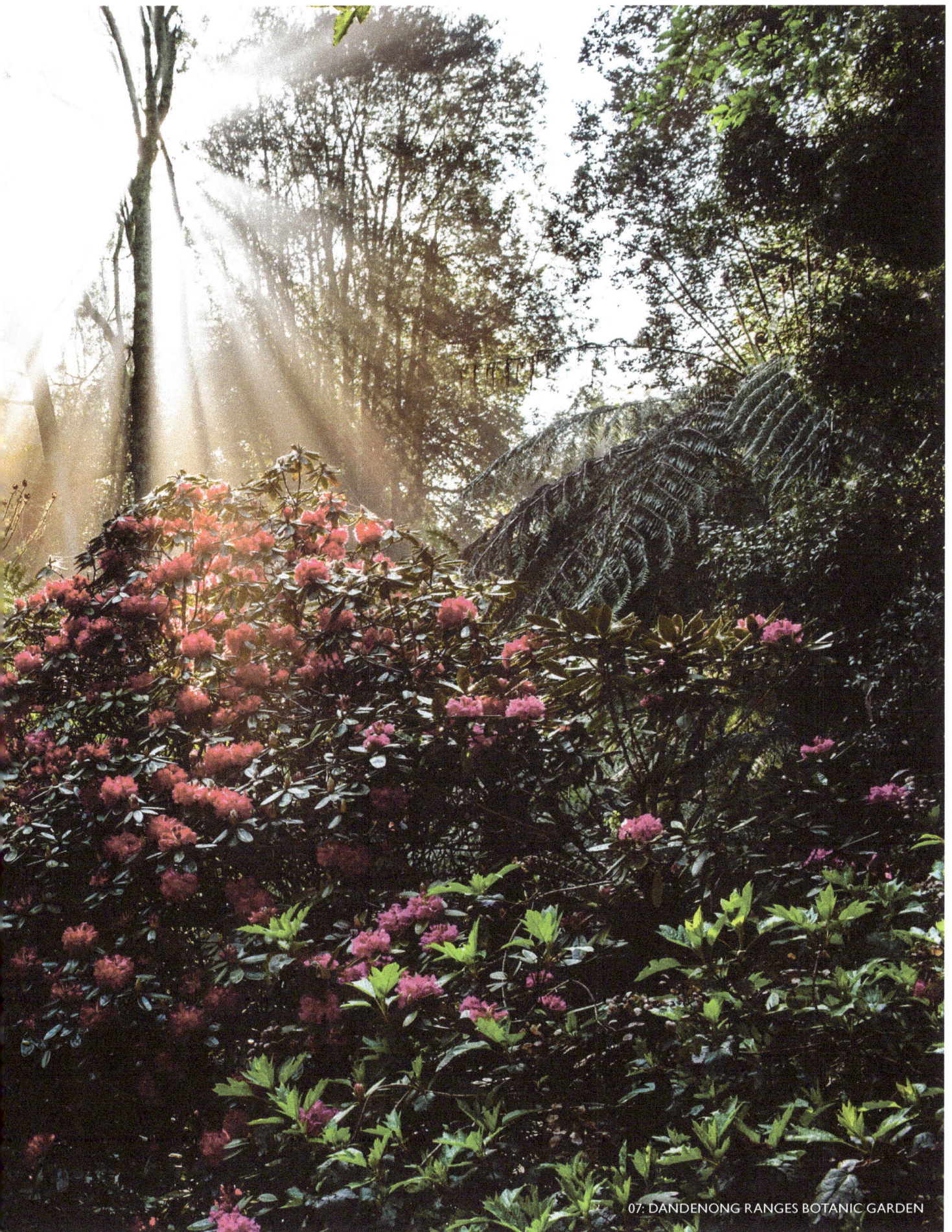

07: DANDENONG RANGES BOTANIC GARDEN

08:

THE EDIBLE FOREST

2164 MELBA HIGHWAY, DIXONS CREEK

What began in 2015 with a simple dream to grow organic vegetables for Yarra Valley Estate's kitchen, became Victoria's largest permaculture food forest. Located on the grounds of Yarra Valley Estate and set over an acre, the Edible Forest has been specifically designed with each plant specifically chosen for its ability to be utilised for food, attract wildlife for pollination, used for healing purposes or enrich the soil.

Guided tours take you through this unique space, where you'll learn about the garden, the plants chosen and their role and discover practical ways to grow and use them at home. Accessible to all, this experience combines sustainability, education, and the simple joy of connecting with nature. Post-tour, browse the onsite nursery to take home a piece of the forest and start your own sustainable garden.

Tour times are booked individually through the website. Group tours are by appointment only. Check website for seasonal time changes.

The Edible Forest is privately owned and maintained.

WHEN: Friday from 2pm to 4pm, Saturday from 10am to 4pm.

COST: Tours are ticketed.

09:
GEORGE TINDALE MEMORIAL GARDEN

33 SHERBROOKE ROAD, SHERBROOKE

The George Tindale Memorial Garden features a selection of plants rarely found in cultivation, but thrive in the acidic soils and shaded, cooler temperate climate of the Dandenong Ranges. Here visitors can enjoy extensive collections of magnolias, rhododendrons, camellias, azaleas and hydrangeas.

Constructed in 1918, the home and garden was purchased by George Tindale in 1958, reflecting his interest in extending knowledge of horticulture. Tindale worked with the Victorian Department of Agriculture as Australia's first full-time cool-storage researcher. The pioneering agricultural scientist created the ornamental garden as his retirement project. Ruth Tindale donated the garden to the Victorian Conservation Trust, in memory of her husband.

Garden enthusiasts can enjoy a gorgeous array of colour each season and stroll the gardens while admiring the permanent sculptures on display, including two from Ruth Tindale. A shady garden lawn offers an ideal spot to bring a picnic and unwind to accompanying birdsong.

George Tindale Memorial Garden is maintained and managed by Parks Victoria.

WHEN: Open daily. Closed Christmas Day.
COST: Free.

09: GEORGE TINDALE MEMORIAL GARDEN

10:
KARWARRA AUSTRALIAN NATIVE BOTANIC GARDENS

1190 - 1192 MOUNT DANDENONG TOURIST ROAD, KALORAMA

The site was originally part of the 1870 selection by Lilydale surveyor Thomas Hand whose family farmed the property until 1939, before being transformed into the botanical garden we know today. Established in 1965, the two-hectare garden features more than 1400 different species of native plants, making it one of the few public gardens exclusively using natives.

Karwarra holds significant conservation responsibilities as it maintains Plant Trust's GPCAA telopea and boronia collections as well as other threatened plants, making it an important repository for endangered Australian flora.

Enjoyable in every season, bring a picnic and settle in amid the boronias, waratahs, native orchids, and plenty more colourful native blooms. The gardens sit at the rear of Kalorama Memorial Reserve where visitors can enjoy electric barbeque facilities, picnic tables and a children's playground. Accessible parking is available at entry with paved pathways for wheelchairs and walkers. Karwarra Australian Native Botanic Gardens is owned and maintained by Yarra Ranges Council.

WHEN: Tuesday to Friday 10am to 4pm, Saturday to Sunday 1pm to 4pm, closed public holidays.

COST: Free.

11:
KURANGA NATIVE NURSERY

118 YORK ROAD, MOUNT EVELYN

Located in the Dandenong Ranges, Kuranga Native Nursery is renowned as an award-winning specialist nursery, showcasing a large range of native plants. Wander through vibrant displays, find rare species, and chat with their expert horticulturalists for ideas to inspire your home garden.

Kuranga Native Nursery offers over 3,500 different species and cultivars, with 70% of them grown onsite.

Explore a diverse range that includes popular varieties such as banksia, boronia, eucalyptus, lilly pilly, wattle, grevillea and kangaroo paw.

More than a garden nursery, browse their gift shop, brimming with Australian-made treasures. Their onsite Paperbark Café, where seasonality and locally-sourced ingredients are enhanced with the unique flavours of Australian bush foods.

Kuranga Native Nursery is privately owned and maintained.

WHEN: Daily from 8:30am to 5pm, cafe closes at 4:30pm. Closed Good Friday and Christmas Day.

COST: Free.

II: KURANGA NATIVE NURSERY

12:

NOBELIUS HERITAGE PARK

5 CRICHTON ROAD, EMERALD

Relocating from Sweden, horticulturalist Carl Petter Nobelius and wife Louisa Amelia, were related to Alfred Bernhard Nobel of Nobel Prize fame. Carl Axel Nobelius was the eldest of their five children and became one of the most renowned nursery proprietors in Australia as founder of Gembrook Nurseries. Once the largest exporter of fruit and ornamental trees in the Southern Hemisphere, exporting to five continents and covering more than 650 hectares at its peak just before WWI, today, Nobelius Heritage Park is heritage listed for its historic significance and offers 4.5 hectares of open space to enjoy walking tracks amid birdlife and lush surroundings. Carl Axel Nobelius was also instrumental in bringing the famous Puffing Billy Railway to the area when he was granted special permission to install a railway siding and packing shed, known as 'Nobelius Station', to service stock exportation. Renowned for the huge selection of mature trees, which are especially spectacular in autumn, visitors can enjoy a garden picnic and take time to visit the Salvia Display Garden, maintained by the Salvia Study Group of Victoria. The 1.4 km Nobelius Track follows the Puffing Billy railway line where strollers enjoy large shady trees mixed with indigenous flora. It's also the location of the Emerald Museum, exhibiting a collection of historical and horticultural artifacts from the Nobelius Nursery dating from the 1880s to the 1960s. Nobelius Heritage Park is maintained and managed by a volunteer committee under the Cardinia Shire Council.

WHEN: Park: Open daily.
            Museum: Wednesday 10am to 3pm; Sunday 12pm to 3pm.

COST: Free.

13:

PIRIANDA GARDEN

5-9 HACKETTS ROAD, OLINDA

In 1959, this was the private garden and home of Harvey and Gillian Ansell prior to the gardens being donated to the Victorian Government in 1977. Set over 11 hectares of terraced woodlands, this unique garden has been designed to take advantage of the steep slopes, with gorgeous views in every season. Paths interlink along stone walls built in the 1960s and early 80s, weaving down to a beautiful fern gully.

Pirianda contains a unique collection of plants, including many botanically important trees, unusual shrubs and perennials including 28 different types of maples and 13 birch varieties. Collections of magnolias, azaleas, rhododendrons, camellias, dogwoods and many conifers can also be seen.

Dogs on a secure lead are welcome. Please note: Visitors should access Hacketts Road via the Olinda-Monbulk Road only. Ignore GPS directions via Perrins Creek Road, as this access is extremely steep and only suitable for 4WD vehicles.

Pirianda Gardens is maintained and managed by Parks Victoria.

WHEN: Open daily.
COST: Free.

14:
R.J. HAMER ARBORETUM

10 CHALET ROAD, OLINDA

Named for the premier of Victoria of 1972 – 1981, Sir Rupert Hamer, the R.J.Hamer Forest Arboretum was originally established to provide a walking and picnicking space within an environment of varied specimens chosen for their interesting flowers and foliage.

The Latin word arboretum means a place for trees and the present-day 101-hectare Arboretum includes over 150 species of native and exotic trees. Unlike a typical arboretum, R.J. Hamer includes rows upon rows of varying species, representing mini-forests that stretch over the rolling hills.

Large plantings of northern hemisphere forest species can be found here, including many from the USA and China. These provide an impressive display of autumn colour. An impressive avenue of Japanese Cedar greets you on entry to the arboretum's main car park.

Visitors enjoy spotting native wildlife and the sweeping views of the Yarra Valley and the Great Dividing Range. Picnic and BBQ areas offer a quiet space to relax and enjoy the views and walking trails. Dogs on leads are welcome within the arboretum's borders, but not permitted in the surrounding national park.

R.J. Hamer Arboretum is maintained and managed by Parks Victoria.

WHEN: Open daily.
COST: Free.

15:

SKYHIGH MOUNT DANDENONG

26 OBSERVATORY ROAD, MOUNT DANDENONG

An ideal spot for garden lovers and family friendly, SkyHigh Mount Dandenong has a variety of gardens to explore including a traditional English garden, a hedged maze, or take a forest walk under a canopy of Australian eucalypts.

Families can enjoy Percy Possums House, the Giant's Chair, Australiana Tree and plenty of space to run.

Enjoy vista views from the SkyHigh Bistro, across Melbourne's city skyline, or bring a picnic and utilise the public barbecues. There are nearby trail walks in the Dandenong Ranges National Park.

A popular location for weddings and functions, SkyHigh also hosts a regular schedule of public festivals and special events on their website.

SkyHigh Mount Dandenong is privately maintained and managed.

WHEN: Open daily, including public holidays.

COST: Free entry, fees apply for maze and parking.

15: SKYHIGH MOUNT DANDENONG

16:

WILLIAM RICKETTS SANCTUARY

1402 MOUNT DANDENONG TOURIST ROAD, MOUNT DANDENONG

William Ricketts Sanctuary, nestled in Victoria's Dandenong Ranges, stands as a testament to the vision of Australian artist William Ricketts (1898–1993). In 1934, Ricketts settled on Mount Dandenong, dedicating his life to creating a series of evocative sculptures that intertwine human forms with the natural environment. His work was profoundly influenced by his time spent with the Pitjantjatjara and Arrernte Aboriginal communities between 1949 and 1960, reflecting his deep respect for Indigenous cultures and their spiritual connection to the land.

In 1961, Ricketts transferred ownership of his property to the Victorian Forests Commission, which subsequently opened it to the public in 1964 as the William Ricketts Sanctuary. The commission provided Ricketts with a new residence, studio, and kiln, allowing him to continue his artistic endeavors on-site until his passing in 1993. The sanctuary features over 90 ceramic sculptures, seamlessly integrated into the lush forest landscape of mountain ash and tree ferns. These artworks depict Indigenous people and wildlife, embodying Ricketts' philosophy of harmony between humans and nature. Visitors can explore the serene grounds, gaining insight into Ricketts' artistic journey and his commitment to environmental and cultural preservation.

WHEN: At time of publication, the site is temporarily closed due to severe storm damage in June 2021. William Ricketts Sanctuary was closed while Parks Victoria carry out the significant and complex work needed to make the site safe for people to enjoy once more. Sections of the sanctuary are planned to be reopened for limited hours once these works are completed, please refer to the Park Victoria website www.parks.vic.gov.au for up to date information.

16: WILLIAM RICKETTS SANCTUARY

Sculpture celebrating Indigenous Elder William Barak.

17:

WURUNDJERI WALK, HEALESVILLE SANCTUARY

GLEN EADIE AVENUE, HEALESVILLE

The self-guided Wurundjeri Walk is accessible to all visitors of Healesville Sanctuary. The garden walk allows visitors to learn more about First Peoples Culture with ample opportunities to stop, reflect and listen to soundscapes from four generations of Elder voices as you meander through the natural bushland setting bursting with colourful flora.

Celebrating the life of Indigenous Elder William Barak, a protector of his people and his culture, the Wurundjeri Walk passes an ancient scar tree, bark canoe, sculpture and a Dreaming Place. Wurundjeri Elder Murrundindi is a regular at the Sanctuary and can guide you along the walk to learn a little language at no added cost. Listen to the sounds of the didgeridoo, hear local stories, and learn about the significance of the local flora.

The Healesville Sanctuary provides an invaluable experience to view native wildlife and support the vital rehabilitation and conservation work done there. The Wurundjeri Walk, Healesville Sanctuary is owned and maintained by Zoos Victoria.

WHEN: Open daily, 9am to 5pm.
COST: Included with Healesville Sanctuary ticket.

Wurundjuri Elder Murrundindi.

18:

YARRA VALLEY ECOSS

711 OLD WARBURTON ROAD, WESBURN

Yarra Valley ECOSS is a Community Environment Hub on Wurundjeri Country committed to showcasing sustainable solutions. They regularly host cultural, educational and musical events as well as seasonal twilight markets and a weekly farmer's market.

Yarra Valley ECOSS also provides residency to a variety of community initiatives whose goals align with a sustainable future, allowing visitors to explore the various art studios, including pottery and woodworking and work on or buy a recycled bike from UpCycles.

Enjoy produce directly from their farm and Organic Shop, buy a native plant at the nursery and enjoy a bite there or BYO picnic and enjoy a rest by the Frog Bog.

With 17 hectares of community gardens and a food forest, there's plenty to explore.

WHEN: Monday to Friday (daylight hours):
Nursery, picnic grounds, community garden volunteering.

Friday 3:30pm to 6pm: ECOSS Valley Market, farm produce, organic shop, food stalls and Mexican cafe.

Weekends: Nursery and events.

COST: Free.

Yarra Valley & Dandenong Ranges

DISCOVER MORE

🔗 visityarravalley.com.au

📷 yarravalleydandenongranges

f VisitYarraValleyandDandenongRanges

FIND YOUR SELF | **MELBOURNE'S YARRA VALLEY AND DANDENONG RANGES**

CREATE YOUR OWN adventure

BLACK SPUR, VICTORIA

VISITOR INFORMATION & TOURING MAP

Discover More with the Yarra Valley & Dandenong Ranges Touring Map!

Your ultimate guide to exploring the best of the region – this beautifully designed map covers both the Yarra Valley and the Dandenong Ranges, helping visitors easily navigate and uncover unforgettable places to stay, eat, and explore.

As the signature print publication from Tourism East Limited, the Touring Map is a must-have for anyone looking to make the most of their visit. Premium and Platinum Partners enjoy featured listings, placing their business front and centre in the hands of thousands of travelers.

Pick up your copy today at key locations throughout the Yarra Valley and Dandenong Ranges – or download and view it online by visiting our website at www.visityarravalley.com.au or scan the QR code.

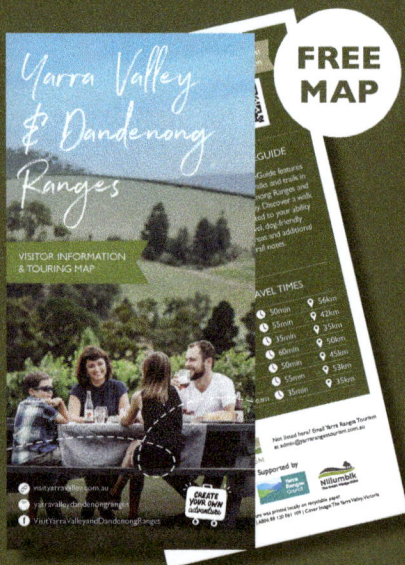

SCAN TO VIEW ONLINE

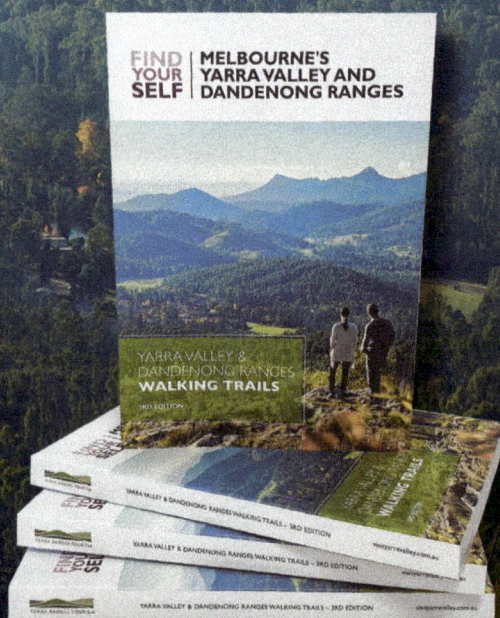